Friends of a Feather

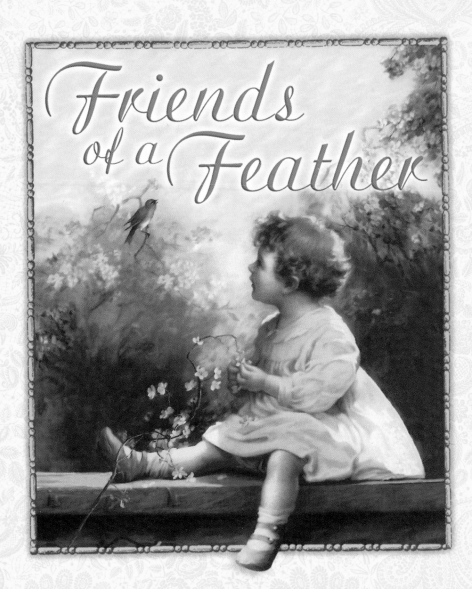

Friends
of a Feather

A Special Gift

for:

_____

from:

_____

date:

_____

I am not of that feather to shake off
My friend when he most need me.

WILLIAM SHAKESPEARE

Cherished Moments
Gift Books

A Basket of Friends

A Feast of Friendship

Leaves of Gold
An Inspirational Classic for our Time

Merry Christmas With Love

Once Upon a Memory
Reflections of Childhood

Seeds of Kindness
Garden Thoughts for the Heart

Strength for a Man's Heart

Sweet Rose of Friendship

Tea for Two
Taking Time for Friends

Where Angels Dwell
*A Treasury of Hope,
Inspiration and Blessing*

Friends
of a Feather

*Featuring the Personal Observations
of Viscount Grey of Fallodon*

Edited by Caroline Brownlow

Brownlow
Brownlow Publishing Company, Inc.

Bird life has many aspects, and each aspect has a peculiar attraction for us. The plumage of birds, infinite in diversity and beauty; their ways on land and water, and especially their ways in the air; their residence or migration; their mating, courtship, and care of their young; the eggs, so plain or so variously marked; the nests, so curiously made, differing so much in structure and in place chosen for them; and above all, the song of birds. Some mammals, reptiles, or insects make noises

that are peculiar to the
mating season, or that
seem to express an emotion
that is pleasant to them;
but the song of birds, the set
performance, variety, and
musical quality, for instance
of a nightingale or a song-
thrush or starling, surpass
similar efforts in all other
orders of life, excepting
only that of mankind.

VISCOUNT GREY

The Sparrow and the Robin

Said the robin to the sparrow,

I should really like to know

Why these anxious human beings

Rush around and worry so.

Said the sparrow to the robin,

Friend, I think that it must be

That they have no heavenly Father

Such as cares for you and me.

Look at the birds of the air; they do not sow or reap or store away in barns, and yet your heavenly Father feeds them. Are you not much more valuable than they?

MATTHEW 6:26

I value my garden more for being full of blackbirds than of cherries, and very frankly give them fruit for their songs.

JOSEPH ADDISON

The true atmosphere of friendship is a sunny one. Griefs and disappointments do not thrive in its clear, healthy light.

RANDOLPH BOURNE

The kingdom of heaven is like a mustard seed, which a man took and planted in his field. Though it is the smallest of all your seeds, yet when it grows, it is the largest of garden plants and becomes a tree, so that the birds of the air come and perch in its branches.

MATTHEW 13:31, 32

There's something so beautiful in coming on one's

very own inmost thoughts in another.

In one way it's one of the greatest pleasures one has.

OLIVE SCHREINER

True friends have no solitary joys or sorrows. Both are shared.

In the hour of peace and gladness, what is our want? Friendship.

When our hearts overflow with gratitude, what is our need? A

friend. When distress haunts us and misery walks by our side,

where do we turn? To friends. Friends to share. Friends to bear.

LEROY BROWNLOW

Empty Nests

Birds sometimes make use of the empty nest of another species, or even use a nest of their own a second time. Two broods of blackbirds were reared in one season in one nest on the Hampshire cottage: whether this was done by one and the same bird or by two different birds I cannot be certain; I assumed it to be done by one bird. After the second brood of blackbirds had left this nest a pair of pied wagtails lined it with a new cup of their own making, and successfully hatched and reared a brood. Three successive broods were thus reared in this one nest in one season. I have known a spotted flycatcher put a new lining in the empty nest of a chaffinch and use this successfully for its own eggs and young.

VISCOUNT GREY

June 6. Another glorious June day. Drove with a large party to Yarningale Common. There were great numbers of birds, chiefly Linnets and Warblers, flitting about the furze, I also noticed a pair of Whin-chats and some Tit-larks. We discovered eight bird's nests in the patches of gorse and bramble—a Yellow Hammer's, two Linnet's, a White-throat's, a Willow Warbler's, a Greenfinch's and two Thrush's. Most of the nests had young ones in, but the Yellow Hammer's contained four eggs.

EDITH HOLDEN

Too many of us stay walled up because we are afraid of being hurt. We are afraid to care too much for fear that the other person does not care at all.

ELEANOR ROOSEVELT

How Sweet the Hedge

How sweet the hedge that hides a cunning nest,

And curtains off a patient bright-eyed thrush,

With five small worlds beneath her mottled breast!

Though life is growing nearer day by day,

Each globe she loves, as yet is mute, and still

Her bosom's beauty slowly wears away.

At last the thin blue veils are backward furled,

Existence wakes and pipes into a bird

As infant music bursts into the world.

And now the mother thrush is proud and gay.

She has her cottage and her pretty young

To feed and lull when western skies turn grey.

NORMAN GALE

*Hearts are linked by God. The friend in whose fidelity
you can count, whose success in life flushes your cheek with
honest satisfaction, whose triumphant career you have
traced and read with a heart-throbbing almost as if it were
a thing alive, for whose honor you would answer as for
your own; that friend, given to you by circumstances
over which you have no control, was God's own gift.*

F. W. ROBERTSON

*Friendship is the comfort of knowing there is always
a shoulder to lean on, a hand to reach out for,
and a heart to welcome me home.*

ANONYMOUS

An Attitude of Joy

There is yet another exhibition of bird happiness
which is neither flight nor sound: it may be
called a joy attitude. A good example of it is to
be seen when a blackbird suns itself on a lawn.
The bird may be observed lying on its side with one wing
uplifted, so that the warm sunshine may penetrate
through the small soft feathers of the body. The appear-
ance is that of a bird ill or wounded or in some distress,
but it is in fact enjoying a sun bath. One of the most
pleasing and attractive sights that I ever beheld was on a

day in June: the air was unusually cold for the time of year and the breeze was chill, but the sun shone full into the chalk-pit close to the Hampshire cottage. I was lingering there to enjoy the warmth of this sheltered sunny place. A family of long-tailed tits flew into the chalk-pit and settled on a young ash tree that rose above the surrounding blackthorns. The little birds were at once conscious of the warmth and disposed themselves in various sun attitudes on the branches of the tree. There they remained, their usually ceaseless activity suspended for a while in motionless enjoyment.

VISCOUNT GREY

I once had a sparrow alight on my shoulder for a moment
while I was hoeing in a village garden, and I felt that
I was more distinguished by that circumstance than
I should have been by any epaulet I could have worn.

HENRY DAVID THOREAU

Be not afraid in misfortune.
When God causes a tree to be hewn down He takes care
that His birds can nestle on another.

ANONYMOUS

We should seize every opportunity to give encouragement.
Encouragement is oxygen to the soul. The days are
always dark enough. There is not need for us to emphasize
the fact by spreading further gloom.

GEORGE M. ADAMS

All Creatures Great and Small

All things bright and beautiful,

All creatures great and small,

All things wise and wonderful,

The Lord God made them all.

Each little flower that opens,

Each little bird that sings,

He made their glowing colors,

He made their tiny wings.

MRS. C. F. ALEXANDER

June 15. The birds still sing morning and evening, but there is not nearly such a full choir as there was a month ago. The cares and responsibilities of large families of hungry fledgelings make too many demands on the time and attention of the anxious parents.

It is very pretty to see the House Martins sitting in the roadway, collecting mud for their nests. Their short-feathered legs look as if they had little white socks on.

EDITH HOLDEN

But I do not lose patience with the birds, however sorely they try me. I love them too well. How should they know that the garden was not planted for them.

CELIA THAXTER

Song of Quiet Contentment

The thrush sings perched in a tree, to which he has mounted for this purpose. There he will maintain his position and his song for some time, especially about dawn and sunset, preferably on the same tree day after day, pausing in his performance as if to select and choose his notes. Probably if birds were to be regarded as endeavouring to please us by song, the thrush should be put first among British birds. He does not rank in the very highest class for quality, but he certainly comes high in the second class. His is undoubtedly a major

song, and owing to the number of thrushes, their persis-

tent singing and the many months in which they are to be

heard, we hear more of their song in the South of England

than that of any other bird, except the robin. In song the

thrush seems to be working very hard to please, and he

succeeds. His song, too, can give a very pleasant impres-

sion of quiet contentment as well as of exultation.

VISCOUNT GREY

If I live by the human equivalents of grace, love, forgiveness and faith with those who occupy space in my life, thinking more of belonging than of owning, seeking to maintain the relationship as a matter of supreme importance, those relationships will never grow "stale," but sweeter every day.

SANDRA W. HOOVER

It is not possible to explain why the blackbird's notes excel and why they mean so much to us. To me there is something in it that I can best describe as intimacy. The songs of other birds please or delight us, but that of the blackbird seems to make a direct appeal to us and stirs some inward emotion.

VISCOUNT GREY

To me, the garden is
a doorway to other worlds;
one of them, of course,
is the world of birds.
The garden is their
dinner table, bursting
with bugs and worms
and succulent berries
(so plant more to
accommodate you both).

ANNE RAVER

My Symphony

To live content with small means; to seek elegance rather than luxury, and refinement rather than fashion; to be worthy, not respectable, and wealthy, not rich; to study hard, think quietly, talk gently, act frankly; to listen to stars and birds, to babes and sages, with open heart; to bear all cheerfully, do all bravely, await occasions, hurry never. In a word, to let the spiritual, unbidden and unconscious, grow up through the common. This is to be my symphony.

WILLIAM ELLERY CHANNING

Shout for joy, O heavens; rejoice, O earth; burst into song, O mountains! For the Lord comforts his people.

ISAIAH 49:13

Letter to a Friend

I salute you. I am your friend and my love for you
goes deep. There is nothing I can give which you have
not got. But there is much, very much, that while
I cannot give it, you can take.

No heaven can come to us unless our hearts find rest in today.
Take heaven! No peace lies in the future which is
not hidden in this present little instance. Take peace!
The gloom of the world is but a shadow.
Behind it, yet within our reach, is joy. Take joy!

Life is so full of meaning and purpose, so full of beauty
that you will find earth but cloaks your heaven.
Courage then to claim it, that is all!

And so I greet you with profound esteem and with
the prayer that for you, now and forever, the day breaks
and the shadows flee away.

FRA GIOVANNI

All sorts of places provide nesting sites for birds:

some nest underground in a hole; others in holes in trees;

others nest on the ground, whether it be on bare earth,

shingle or rock, or in grass or heather; others nest in bushes

or trees; and some, such as swifts, swallows,

and house martins, have become dependent on

the buildings of mankind.

NED ROREN

In his hand is the life of every creature

and the breath of all mankind.

JOB 12:10

Sooner or later you've heard all your best friends have to say.

Then comes the tolerance of real love.

NED ROREN

She Is My Friend

She is my friend! The words

Brought Summer and the birds;

And all my Winter time

Thawed into running rhyme

And rippled into song,

Warm, tender, brave and strong.

And so it sings today—

So may it sing alway!

Let each mute measure end

With "Still she is my friend."

Riley

In contrast to the tendency to save labour in nest-building by using a ready-made nest, some birds build more nests than are ever used for their own eggs. The moorhen, for instance, makes several nests. In this case it seems as if the birds felt bound to do more than once what can be done so easily.

VISCOUNT GREY

Offer hospitality to one another… Each one should use whatever gift he has received to serve others.

1 PETER 4:9, 10

It is great to have friends when one is young, but indeed it is still more so when you are getting old. When we are young, friends are, like everything else, a matter of course. In the old days we know what it means to have them.

EDWARD GRIEG

A Summer Song

In July we hear the last spring song of the thrush and robin.
To listen to the last of either of these two birds is not, however,
so melancholy a matter as to hear the last blackbird's song.
The robin and the thrush will be heard again soon: the
blackbird will not be heard till February: the leaves must
change colour and fall, the days get dark and short and then
lengthen again; the worst severity of winter must be endured
before we hear those moving notes once more.

VISCOUNT GREY

Use the talents you have; for the woods would be silent
if no birds sang except the best.

I think if it's at all possible, your best friend and you owe it to each other to make some space just to be alone together again. That way, you can talk about what you were, and that feels good. You can also talk about what you are—that's trickier, but if you're lucky, that feels good too.

ELIZABETH BERG

Morning is the best of all times in the garden. The sun is not yet hot. Sweet vapors rise from the earth. Night dew clings to the soil and makes plants glisten. Birds call to one another. Bees are already at work.

WILLIAM LONGGOOD

What It Means to Be a Friend

I love you not only for what you are,

but for what I am when I am with you.

I love you not only for what you have made of yourself,

but for what you are making of me.

I love you for the part of me that you bring out.

I love you for putting your hand into my heaped-up heart,

and passing over all the foolish and frivolous and weak things

which you cannot help dimly seeing there, and for drawing

out into the light all the beautiful, radiant belongings,

that no one else had looked quite far enough to find.

I love you for ignoring the possibilities of the fool and weakling in me, and for laying firm hold on the possibilities of good in me. I love you for closing your eyes to the discords in me, and for adding to the music in me by worshipful listening.

I love you because you are helping me to make of the lumber of my life not a tavern but a Temple, and of the words of my every day not a reproach but a song.

I love you because you have done more than any creed could have done to make me good, and more than any fate could have done to make me happy. You have done it just by being yourself. Perhaps that is what being a friend means after all.

Friend of Mine

I'd like to be the sort of friend that you have been to me;

I'd like to be the help that you've been always glad to be;

I'd like to mean as much to you each minute of the day

As you have meant, old friend of mine, to me along the way.

EDGAR A. GUEST

Praise the Lord from the earth,

you mountains and all hills,

fruit trees and all cedars,

wild animals and all cattle,

small creatures and flying birds.

PSALM 148:7, 9, 10

October 3. The Swifts have all disappeared and for some days I have not seen any Martins flying about. Long before I left Perthshire, every morning I used to watch the House Martins from my bed-room window, collecting in great flocks on the house-roofs, preparatory to their departure.

There are still some Swallows to be seen, but the greater number have gone South. The Robins are beginning to sing again.

EDITH HOLDEN

May you be richly rewarded by the Lord, the God of Israel, under whose wings you have come to take refuge.

RUTH 2:12

To Each Her Nest

The varieties and peculiarities of nests and of sites chosen for them are very great. Sometimes the reason for the peculiarity is apparent. For instance, the cup of the reed-warbler's nest is unusually deep: the nest is woven on to the stems of the reeds and is tilted when the reeds are swayed in a strong wind: the depth of the cup lessens the risk of the eggs being rolled out of the nest. Here there is a reason for the peculiarity of the reed-warbler's nest satisfactory to our intelligence; but many variations in nest-building provoke questions that leave us puzzled and silent. Some warblers line their nests profusely with feathers, and the whole structure is designed for warmth: but the blackcap and garden-warbler get on very well with the thinnest possible open nest, with no warm lining. So thin is a blackcap's nest that the eggs can sometimes be seen through the bottom of the nest by one looking up from below. The blackcap is an example of great economy in the use of material; it is a wonder that out of such little material a cup can be built that will hold eggs at all.

VISCOUNT GREY

The Power of Kindness

Without love and kindness,

life is cold, selfish, and uninteresting,

and leads to distaste for everything.

With kindness, the difficult becomes easy,

the obscure clear; life assumes a charm

and its miseries are softened. If we knew

the power of kindness, we should

transform this world into a paradise.

CHARLES WAGNER

Eggs are interesting, curious, and often beautiful; but more wonderful are nests. I suppose it must be said that birds choose a site and build a nest by instinct and not by intelligence; for each bird that builds a nest for the first time does this after the manner of its kind, without teaching or experience to bring the faculty of reason into action. Instinct, then, must have the credit of what is done, but the result is wonderful.

VISCOUNT GREY

I think that love is the only spiritual power that can overcome the self-centeredness that is inherent in being alive. Love is the thing that makes life possible or, indeed, tolerable.

ARNOLD TOYNBEE

God
gives every
bird
his food,
but He
does not
throw it
into
the nest.

JOSIAH GILBERT HOLLAND

October 21. The last of our Summer visitants has taken his departure. About a fortnight ago a Chiff-Chaff was constantly to be seen hopping about the Gooseberry bushes in the garden;— the last to leave us, he is usually the first to arrive. But the Tom-tits are returning in great numbers to their old haunts in the garden, which they have deserted during the summer. They flutter about the wall and the windows of the house, I believe with a secret hope of finding a Cocoa-nut waiting for them.

EDITH HOLDEN

How Great Thou Art

When through the woods and forest glades I wander

And hear the birds sing sweetly in the trees;

When I look down from lofty mountain grandeur

And hear the brook and feel the gentle breeze;

Then sings my soul, my Savior God to Thee;

How great Thou art, how great Thou art!

STUART K. HINE

If wisdom were given me under the express condition

that it must be kept hidden and not uttered,

I should refuse it. No good thing is pleasant to possess,

without friends to share it.

SENECA

I Shall Not Live in Vain

If I can stop one heart from breaking,

I shall not live in vain:

If I can ease one life the aching,

Or cool one pain,

Or help one fainting robin

Unto his nest again,

I shall not live in vain.

EMILY DICKINSON

In the Meadow

While ripening corn grew thick and deep,

And here and there men stood to reap,

One morn I put my heart to sleep,

And to the meadows took my way.

The goldfinch on a thistle-head

Stood scattering seedlets as she fed,

The wrens their pretty gossip spread,

Or joined a random roundelay.

JEAN INGELOW

I trust that even when I'm out of sight I'm not

out of mind. Silences and distances are woven into

the texture of every true friendship.

ROBERTA ISRAELOFF

December 30. The frost still holds,
Snow lightly throughout the day. The birds
have become wonderfully bold this last week since
their usual hunting-grounds have been buried in
snow. The Blackbirds and Thrushes are usually
rather shy, and fly away at the approach of
anyone, but now they only hop away to a little
distance and sit watching with their bright eyes,
from beneath the friendly shelter of a bush,
waiting to go back to their feast of crumbs.

EDITH HOLDEN

Illustration Credits

Brownlow Collection: Pages 1, 3, 5, 6, 24, 31, 43, 46, 50, 53.

Thomas L. Cathey: Pages 8, 14, 16, 20-21, 22, 30, 44-45, 47.

Fine Art Images: Pages 35, 48.

Fine Art Photographic Library: Pages 7, 9, 10-11, 14, 15, 19, 25, 27, 32-33, 37, 41, 54-55, 56, 58, 62.